# Cinco de Mayo

A Proud Heritage The Hispanic Library

# Cinco de Mayo

*A Mexican Holiday about Unity and Pride*

James Garcia

The
Child's
World

Published in the United States of America by The Child's World®
PO Box 326 • Chanhassen, MN 55317-0326 • 800-599-READ • www.childsworld.com

Acknowledgments
   The Creative Spark: Mary Francis-DeMarois, Project Director; Carrie Nichols Cantor, Series
   Editor; Robert Court, Design and Art Direction
   Carmen Blanco, Curriculum Adviser
   The Child's World®: Mary Berendes, Publishing Director

Photos
   AP/Wide World Photos: 16; Archivo Iconografico, S.A./CORBIS: 9; Morton Beebe/CORBIS:
   30; Neil Beer/CORBIS: 28; Bettmann/CORBIS: 8; Jonathan Blair/CORBIS: 13; Phil Cantor: 21,
   26; Corbis: 15, 24, 25; Richard Cummins/CORBIS: 20; Philip Gould/CORBIS: 35; Institute of
   Texan Cultures: 10, 32; Catherine Karnow/CORBIS: 18; Charles & Josette Lenars/CORBIS:
   22; Los Angeles Public Library: 19; Reuters NewMedia Inc./CORBIS: 33; Judith Rew: 7; Texas
   Department of Transportation: cover; University of Texas at Austin General Libraries: 12

Library of Congress Cataloging-in-Publication Data
   Garcia, James.
     Cinco de mayo : a Mexican holiday about unity and pride / by James Garcia.
         p. cm. — (Proud heritage)
   Includes bibliographical references and index.
       ISBN 1-56766-174-2 (library bound : alk. paper)
     1.  Cinco de Mayo (Mexican holiday)—Juvenile literature. 2. Mexico—Social life and
   customs—Juvenile literature.  I. Title: 5 de mayo. II. Title. III. Series: Proud heritage
   (Child's World)
     F1233 .G232 2002
     394.26972—dc21

                                                      2002005074

# The History behind Cinco de Mayo

*Cinco de Mayo* (pronounced SINK-oh duh MY-oh) is Spanish for "Fifth of May." That day in 1862 was the date of an important battle in which Mexican forces defeated France. It was called the Battle of Puebla. Mexicans celebrate this day every year, much as Americans celebrate Memorial Day.

How did the war between France and Mexico start? It began as a problem over money. In 1861, Mexico's president Benito Juárez decided to stop repaying money that Mexico owed to European governments. Juárez, a Zapotec Indian, had just been elected to his second term as president. Juárez believed that Mexico was too poor to continue paying its debts. He believed he had no choice but to stop making payments on his country's debt for two years.

## Invading Mexico

The leaders of England, France, and Spain were angry at the Mexican president's decision. They wanted their money. They decided to punish Juárez by invading Mexico. The armies of all three nations landed in Veracruz, on the eastern shore of Mexico, in December

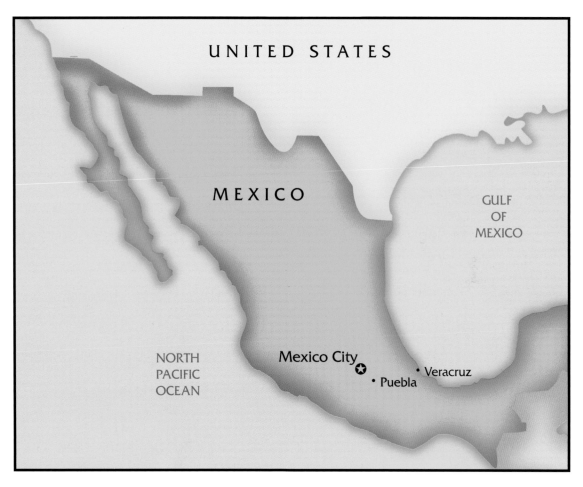

*Mexico's borders in the 1860s were the same as they are today. The Battle of Puebla took place in the town of Puebla in the southern part of Mexico, west of the coastal city of Veracruz.*

*Napoléon III, the nephew of the famous French emperor Napoléon Bonaparte, was not willing to forgive Mexico's debts. He sent troops to conquer Mexico.*

1861. But the leaders of England and Spain soon changed their minds and ordered their troops to return home.

The French, however, decided to go ahead with their plan to take control of Mexico. France's ruler, Emperor Napoléon III (nephew of the famous Napoléon Bonaparte), hoped to expand France's power in the Americas by invading Mexico. He also wanted to keep the United States from growing more powerful.

When he heard about the French invasion, President Juárez sent an army to fight back in the Mexican town of Puebla. The French were shocked when they saw how hard the Mexicans fought in Puebla. After only one day of battle, the Mexicans forced the French to **retreat.** Word of the Mexican army's unexpected victory quickly spread across the country.

Although many men had been killed or wounded, the French army was not completely defeated. The French general called on Emperor Napoléon to send more fighters to help. Angry and embarrassed by the defeat, Napoléon ordered 30,000 more troops to Mexico. The French army was able to take over the capital, Mexico City. President

*This engraving shows the French attack on Puebla, with Fort Guadalupe in the background.*

*Archduke Maximilian of Austria was appointed emperor of Mexico in 1832.*

Juárez fled to northern Mexico to rebuild his army. In 1832, Napoléon appointed an Austrian, Ferdinand Maximilian, to serve as the new emperor of Mexico.

U.S. president Abraham Lincoln was troubled by France's invasion of Mexico. Forty years earlier, President James Monroe had vowed not to permit Europeans to gain power in the Americas. His promise was called the Monroe Doctrine. But for now, there was little the United States could do. It had its own problems. Its Northern states were fighting its Southern states in the Civil War (1861–1865). President Lincoln was afraid that if he helped Mexico, France would help the Southern states win the Civil War.

Finally, though, when the Civil War was over, the U.S. government began to send money and other aid to Mexico. Several thousand U.S. troops went south of the border to help the Mexicans get rid of Emperor Maximilian. In 1867, Maximilian was captured and killed.

Despite the French army's later victories, the Mexican victory at Puebla was considered important. It was a big event in the Mexican nation's struggle for independence. Mexicans and Mexican Americans celebrate the Battle of Puebla to honor their unity, patriotism, bravery, and independence.

Benito Juárez is often called the Abraham Lincoln of Mexico because he fought to keep his country independent and united. He worked all of his life against unfairness and **corruption** in Mexico. Like Lincoln, Juárez grew up poor. He was born to Zapotec Indian farmers in the Oaxaca village of San Pablo Gueletao on March 21, 1806.

When Juárez was 13, he went to Oaxaca City with his sister, who worked as a servant for a family. He could not read, write, or speak Spanish. The family took Juárez in and educated him.

Juárez was a hard worker. He learned very quickly, too. He impressed his teachers so much that they sent him to a Franciscan school in Oaxaca to become a priest. Juárez, however, decided to study law instead of religion. After graduating from the seminary, he went on to another school to become a lawyer.

Many lawyers go into politics. Juárez began his political career as governor of Oaxaca from 1847 to 1852. Then he was forced to leave Mexico because he spoke out against the dictator who had made himself president. He played an important role in a revolution that overthrew the government in Mexico.

Juárez became the minister of justice in the new government in 1854. Two years later, he became president.

Juárez is known for his great courage and honesty. Most of Mexico's rulers before him had been selfish, dishonest, and violent. Juárez upheld the law during a time of upheaval. He opposed allowing only rich people, churchmen, and soldiers to have all the best things in Mexico. He never gave up his dream of making his country a good place for everyone. Benito Juárez died of a heart attack on July 18, 1872.

# Celebrating Cinco de Mayo

In Mexico, Cinco de Mayo is celebrated with events organized by the Mexican government. Soldiers march in parades. Serious ceremonies honor the soldiers who gave their lives at the Battle of Puebla. People dress up like 19th-century soldiers and **reenact** the famous battle. Some of the events are like those held in the United States on Veterans Day and Memorial Day, which honor soldiers who fought in America's wars.

More than 20 million people in the United States were born in Mexico or have ancestors who came from Mexico. They like to celebrate Cinco de Mayo, too. Mexican Americans celebrate Cinco de Mayo differently from people in Mexico. The partying is often more lively and fun in the United States. There are noisy, colorful festivals with lots of Mexican foods, folk dancing, and music. A Cinco de Mayo festival in America often

*This photograph shows a Cinco de Mayo celebration in Mexico City in 1885. At this time, many people were alive who still remembered the Battle of Puebla.*

includes Latin music bands and theater, many children's activities, and even carnival rides.

Until recently, only Mexicans and Mexican Americans celebrated Cinco de Mayo. But the growing popularity of Latino food and culture across the country has meant that many others are also enjoying the holiday. Cinco de Mayo festivals in cities such as Los Angeles, Houston, Chicago, and San Antonio attract large and **diverse** crowds, just as St. Patrick's Day is celebrated by many people with no link to Ireland.

The popularity of Cinco de Mayo in the United States is expected to grow. Most immigrants to the United States in the past ten years have come from Mexico. Meanwhile, many more Americans have begun to enjoy and celebrate Latino culture.

*Every year Cinco de Mayo is celebrated in some places with a reenactment of the Battle of Puebla. Actors dress up as French soldiers and Mexican defenders.*

Since the 1500s, thousands of Mexican families lived in what we now call New Mexico, Texas, Arizona, California, Colorado, and Utah. After a war between the United States and Mexico called the Mexican War (1846–1848), this area became part of the United States. The Mexican families who lived there became Americans. Thousands of immigrants move to the United States from Mexico every year. Some risk their lives to come illegally.

States with large Mexican populations, such as Texas, New Mexico, Arizona, California, Colorado, and Illinois, hold the largest Cinco de Mayo celebrations in the United States. In Texas and California, about one out of every five people is of Mexican origin. More and more Mexicans are living in such states as Florida, Nevada, North Carolina, Georgia, Indiana, and Ohio. Cinco de Mayo fiestas are now held in many cities throughout the United States.

## Celebration in Los Angeles

The largest Cinco de Mayo celebration in the United States is held in Los Angeles, California. More than 500,000 people

*Cinco de Mayo is a much-loved holiday. Celebrations in large cities like New York and Los Angeles are huge.*

participate in the **festivities** there every year. Almost half of the people who live in Los Angeles County are Hispanic. Los Angeles has more Mexicans and Mexican Americans than any other city in the United States.

The city of Los Angeles has several Cinco de Mayo celebrations. The biggest and best-known fiesta takes place on Olvera Street, which is in the oldest part of the city. More than 200 years ago, Spanish settlers established the city of Los Angeles right on what is now Olvera Street. Today, the street is home to 27 historic buildings, a traditional Mexican plaza, and a church that was built in 1784. Cinco de Mayo on Olvera Street features a parade, live music and dance performances, and mounds of wonderful Mexican food.

*Olvera Street in Los Angeles is where the first Spanish settlers lived when the city was founded. Many tourists go there today to eat Mexican food and shop in its charming outdoor market.*

*These dancers performed at a Cinco de Mayo festival in San Diego.*

Thousands of people of all backgrounds come to Olvera Street every Cinco de Mayo. The colorful festival has become an American tradition.

Cinco de Mayo is also celebrated at schools and parks across the United States. Many schools provide *baile folkloric* (folk dancing) performances, and cafeterias offer a Mexican menu for the holiday. All people who celebrate this wonderful holiday will find that it has even more meaning when they understand its history.

# Chapter Three

# Making Your Own Fiesta

You don't have to attend a big-city fiesta to celebrate Cinco de Mayo. Anyone can enjoy this colorful holiday right in the backyard. Like other parties, Cinco de Mayo fiestas require three important things: food, crafts, and music.

Cinco de Mayo celebrations in the United States usually revolve around food. Mexican food is a mixture of traditional Native American and Spanish foods. In Mexico, some of the most common dishes are tacos and tostadas.

*The seeds are the hottest part of a chili. Chilies are a key ingredient in many Mexican dishes.*

*Typical Mexican dishes are made using tortillas, tacos, beans, avocados, different kinds of peppers, onions, garlic, and tomatoes, just to name a few of the main ingredients.*

Mexican restaurants in the United States have developed other dishes, such as burritos and nachos.

The most popular Mexican dishes use corn or flour tortillas, which are rolled, folded, fried, or toasted. Mexicans eat tortillas instead of bread. A hot tortilla right off the griddle is as tasty as hot bread out of the oven.

Many Mexican dishes also use chilies as a key ingredient. Chilies are peppers. They can be mild, medium, hot, or very hot. They are grown on vines or bushes and come in many different colors and sizes. Some are red and yellow. Others, like jalapeños, are green and fiery hot. Chilies are used in salsas, gravies, and sauces.

For your Cinco de Mayo fiesta, pick one or two dishes you like to make. Be certain you have on hand lots of tortilla chips and guacamole!

## Recipes

Here are some simple recipes for a Mexican celebration. This is a great dip for tortilla chips:

Guacamole

You will need:
2 ripe avocados
1 small tomato, chopped
1 tablespoon minced onion

a dash or two of garlic powder
salt and pepper to taste

Halve the avocados and remove the pit. With a spoon, scoop out the pulp and mash with a fork. Add the other ingredients, mix well, and put in a serving dish. Serve with tortilla chips. Serves about four.

# Nachos are always popular. Here's an easy recipe:

## Nachos

You will need:

| | |
|---|---|
| *1 tablespoon olive oil* | *12 ounce can of refried beans* |
| *1 pound of ground beef* | *1 cup sour cream* |
| *taco seasoning mix* | *sliced Jalapeño peppers* |
| *large bag of taco chips* | *chopped scallions* |
| *12 ounce jar of nacho cheese* | *chopped black olives* |

Heat the olive oil in a sauté pan. Cook the ground beef in the pan, and mix in the taco seasoning. Spread out the taco chips on a platter. Put the beans and nacho cheese each in a separate saucepan and heat them up on the stove until hot and bubbly. (Alternatively, you can put them in microwave-safe containers and heat them in a microwave.) Spoon the meat and beans over the chips. Then pour the cheese on top. Add any or all of the other ingredients on top. Serves about eight.

Tacos and burritos are another easy dish. Here are instructions:

## Tacos and Burritos

You will need:

| | |
|---|---|
| 1 tablespoon olive oil | head of lettuce, shredded |
| 1 pound ground beef | 8 ounces cheddar or Monterey Jack |
| taco seasoning mix | cheese, shredded |
| 12 tortillas, corn and/or flour | 1 small onion, chopped |
| 2 tomatoes, diced | cilantro, chopped |

Heat the olive oil in a sauté pan. Brown the beef and mix in the taco seasoning. Heat up the corn or flour tortillas on a griddle and stack them in a covered dish to keep them warm.

Place all the food on the table and let your guests fill their tortillas with beef and any of the other goodies. For tacos, they'll just fold their corn or flour tortillas in half. Burritos are made using larger flour tortillas. They should fold in the top and bottom of the tortilla and then roll it up, being careful to keep the ingredients in the middle. Serves about six.

*These paper flowers are fun and easy to make.*

## Crafts

If you really want to create a festive Cinco de Mayo atmosphere, add some Mexican crafts to your celebration. You can make them ahead of time or have the materials ready so that your guests have the fun of doing it themselves.

Mexican flowers are easy and fun to make. Here's how:

### Mexican Flowers

You will need:

4 sheets colorful tissue paper for each flower (6-by-12-inch paper works well)

2 green pipe cleaners for each flower

perfume (optional)

You'll be folding the paper to make a fan. Place all four sheets right on top of one another. Fold them lengthwise and as though they are one piece. Starting at the bottom, fold 1 inch of the tissue paper up and away from you. Then fold that whole section toward you. Continue folding back and forth until all the tissue paper is folded up into a 1-inch-wide strip that is 12 inches long.

Now, attach the two pipe cleaners at one end so that you have an extra-long one. Bend the double pipe cleaner into a V shape. Squeeze the paper fan at its middle. Twist the middle of the pipe cleaner tightly around it. Twist the two halves of the pipe cleaner around each other to form the stalk. To make the petals, pull the paper sheets apart and forward. When you're finished with all the layers, spray a light mist of perfume on it.

Want a place to put all those pretty flowers? Why not make Mexican flowerpots? To the right are the instructions:

## Music and Dance

Your Cinco de Mayo celebration must also include traditional Mexican music. Mariachi music is traditional folk

> **Mexican Flowerpots**
>
> You will need:
> *brightly colored paints*
> *paintbrushes*
> *small terracotta pots*
> *yarn and ribbon (optional)*
>
> Let your imagination run wild. Paint stripes, zigzag patterns, flowers, animals, or anything you can think of on the pots. For a more festive look, dress up the pots with strips of yarn and ribbon.

music often performed during Cinco de Mayo and other Mexican celebrations. A mariachi band can include as few as three members or as many as 20. The band usually includes a large, hand-held bass guitar known as a *guitarro bajo sexto* (gee-TA-ro BA-ho SEX-toh), a small guitar called a *vihuela* (vee-HWAY-la), and trumpets. The music is believed to have originated in the Mexican state of Jalisco. It is a lively blend of orchestra and folk sounds. The songs are mostly **ballads** sung with theatrical flare.

Cinco de Mayo fiestas also feature a lot of dancing. Mexican folk dances include the *zapateado* (zah-PAH-tay-AH-doe), a dance that originated in Spain. In this dance, performers tap the heels of their shoes hard against a

*Mariachi bands are very common in Mexico. In restaurants, the musicians will come and play for each table.*

dance floor. The most popular zapateado associated with Cinco de Mayo is known as the Mexican hat dance.

Male and female performers dance difficult and rapid steps around a Mexican sombrero set on the floor. Sometimes dancers compete to see who can perform the quickest and most **elaborate** steps around the hat. Female folkloric dancers wear vibrant costumes with long ruffled

One of the most popular Mexican folk songs became a hit twice in the United States. Richie Valens made the song popular in the United States by turning it into a rock song in the 1950s. Many years later, the band Los Lobos spiced it up when they recorded it for the soundtrack for *La Bamba,* the 1987 movie about Richie Valens's life. Here are some of the lyrics of the song "La Bamba."

*Para bailar la Bamba* (In order to dance the Bamba)

*Para bailar la Bamba* (In order to dance the Bamba)

*Se necesita una poca de gracia* (A little bit of grace is needed)

*Una poca de gracia* (A little bit of grace)

*Pa mi y pa ti* (For me and for you)

*Ahi arriba ahi arriba* (Ah higher and higher)

*Ahi arriba ahi arriba* (Ah higher and higher)

*Por ti sere* (For you I'll be)

*Por ti sere* (For you I'll be)

*Yo no soy marinero* (I am not a sailor)

*Yo no soy marinero* (I am not a sailor)

*Soy capitan soy capitan* (I'm a captain, I'm a captain.)

*Bamba Bamba Bamba Bamba*

*Bamba Bamba Bamba*

*The dresses that girls wear to dance Mexican folk dances are colorful and festive.*

skirts that seem to be made from swaths of colorful ribbon. The women hold the skirts in their hands and make colorful patterns in the air with their dance steps.

Traditional dance, music, and food make up almost every Cinco de Mayo celebration. Combining all of these is what makes the holiday so much fun.

# The Meaning of Cinco de Mayo

Cinco de Mayo has become so popular across the country, it is even celebrated at the White House. On May 5, 2001, President George W. Bush and his wife, Laura, hosted the first-ever Cinco de Mayo fiesta on the South Lawn of the White House. It was a star-studded event with about 300 guests. The White House celebration included a traditional mariachi band, a colorfully dressed Mexican folkloric dance group, and pop singer Thalia.

President Bush delivered a special speech for Cinco de Mayo in English and Spanish—another first for a U.S. president. He said: "May fifth marks the triumph of the spirit of freedom for the people of Mexico. The victory of General Ignacio Zaragoza [the leader of the Mexican force fighting at Puebla] and his Mexican troops over the superior French forces at the Battle of Puebla served as a stirring reminder of the determination to win the fight for

*General Ignacio Zaragoza led the Mexican forces to victory against the French at the Battle of Puebla. He is considered a Mexican national hero. Many schools, plazas, and streets are named after him.*

Mexico's freedom from **foreign intervention.** The Cinco de Mayo display of courage and purpose is a source of pride for all freedom-loving people.

"We Americans cherish our deep historical, cultural, economic, and, in many cases, family ties with Mexico and Latin America. Cinco de Mayo celebrations remind us how much Hispanics have influenced and enriched the United States."

Cinco de Mayo has meaning to all kinds of people, not only to Mexicans. The holiday is about more than just a historical event in which the Mexicans defeated the French in a battle at Puebla. For many it is about living life with

*On May 5, 2001, President George W. Bush held the first-ever Cinco de Mayo celebration at the White House.*

pride and courage. It is about the importance of standing together to achieve goals.

## Different Meanings to Different People

Writer Victor Garcia believes, "Cinco de Mayo symbolizes the struggle for **sovereignty,** self-determination, and commitment to fight even when the odds seem insurmountable."

People who believe in a traditional Cinco de Mayo sometimes complain that it is not properly celebrated in the United States. They say it is because many people don't know the history behind the holiday. They don't know about the Battle of Puebla, fought between France and Mexico on May 5, 1862. Some people mistakenly believe that Cinco de Mayo marks the anniversary of Mexico's independence from Spain.

The Mexican holiday most like the Fourth of July celebration in the United States is *Diez y Seis de Septiembre* (September 16). That holiday celebrates the anniversary of the start of the war Mexicans fought between 1810 and 1821 to gain their freedom from Spain. Mexico's revolution occurred 36 years after Americans fought to gain their freedom from England.

Roberto Vargas, a parent in California, sees Cinco de Mayo in much the same way. He also believes the celebration represents a duty to fight for what is right. He explains that Mexican-American college students during the 1970s began celebrating Cinco de Mayo as "a popular community event, using it to teach the importance of continuing to fight for justice, despite the obstacles."

*These Mexican girls are jumping rope in front of a mural that depicts the heroes and villains of Cinco de Mayo.*

Gabriel Buelna, a college professor, says Cinco de Mayo is viewed by many people as the anniversary of an event that showed that "Mexico could hold its own against other better-armed enemies."

Author Robert Con Davis-Undiano believes Cinco de Mayo simply means, "I'm still standing—don't count me out."

Asked to describe what Cinco de Mayo means to him, sixth-grader Peter Robledo says, "It shows it doesn't matter if you're outnumbered. You can still win."

Fidel Montoya, a parent in Colorado, sums it up as follows: "It's a day to acknowledge our cultural and historical ties to Mexico. It's a day to reflect about Mexico's glorious past and its hope for the future. It's also a day when we as Americans can appreciate the cultural and historical contributions of significance made by Mexico. Cinco de Mayo is a day to enjoy and celebrate."

## Celebrate Cinco de Mayo

How about having a really special Cinco de Mayo this year? You can go to a big fiesta or invite friends over for your own party at home. Make tacos, listen to Mariachi music, and hand out sombreros. But while you're having fun, be sure to remember the heroic soldiers who lost their lives at the Battle of Puebla defending Mexico from foreign invaders. Think of all the times people have had to fight to remain free, in Mexico, in the United States, and around the world.

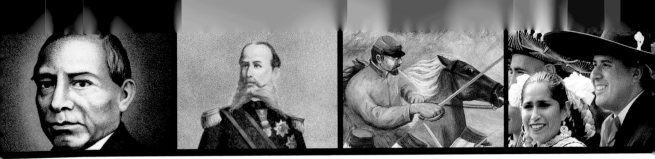

**1806:** Benito Juárez is born on March 21 in the Oaxaca village of San Pablo Gueletao.

**1810:** Mexico launches its 11-year war for independence against Spain.

**1821:** Mexico wins independence from Spain. For many years afterwards various groups in Mexico battle against each other for control of the country.

**1836:** Texas wins independence from Mexico.

**1846:** War breaks out between the United States and Mexico.

**1847:** Benito Juárez becomes governor of Oaxaca.

**1858:** Benito Juárez becomes president of Mexico.

**1861:** The U.S. Civil War begins. France, Spain, and Britain send troops to Mexico to collect on outstanding debts. Spain and Britain change their minds and send their troops home. France decides to stay and take over the country.

**1862:** Mexico's army defeats French invasion on May 5 at the Battle of Puebla, but cannot prevent the French from taking over the country. President Juárez flees to northern Mexico to avoid capture by French troops.

**1864:** France's emperor, Napoléon III, appoints Austrian archduke Ferdinand Maximilian to serve as emperor of Mexico. Maximilian and his wife, Carlota, rule for three years.

**1865:** The U.S. Civil War ends. American troops join the Mexican army in its war for independence against France.

**1867:** Mexican army defeats the French. Benito Juárez regains the presidency of Mexico.

**1872:** Benito Juárez dies on July 18.

**2001:** First Cinco de Mayo celebration is held at the White House.

**ballads (BAL-ledz)** Ballads are romantic or sentimental songs. At Cinco de Mayo festivals mariachi bands often play slow, romantic ballads first sung in Mexico in the 1800s.

**corruption (kuh-RUP-shun)** Corruption is dishonest or unfair behavior. One of Mexico's most famous presidents, Benito Juárez, fought against corruption in his country's government.

**diverse (dih-VERSS)** If something is diverse it has many different qualities. If a group of people is diverse it includes people who are not all the same. The people who attend Cinco de Mayo festivals in cities like Los Angeles, California are diverse because they are from many different backgrounds.

**elaborate (eh-LA-ber-it)** If something is elaborate it is complicated and includes a lot of details. Mexican folk dances often require dancers to perform many elaborate steps.

**festivities (fess-TIH-vih-teez)** Festivities are joyful celebrations. Cinco de Mayo festivities in the United States remind people of the brave heroes who fought at the Battle of Puebla in 1862.

**foreign intervention (FOR-en in-ter-VEN-shun)** Foreign intervention is when one country gets involved in the affairs of another country. When the French army invaded Mexico in 1862 that was considered an act of foreign intervention. The United States objected to France's foreign intervention in Mexico and later helped the Mexican army defeat the French invaders.

**reenact (ree-en-AKT)** To reenact an event is to perform that act again. People sometimes dress up like the soldiers who fought at the Battle of Puebla to reenact that famous historical event.

**retreat (ree-TREET)** To retreat means to back away, as when an army moves backwards during a battle that it is losing. The French army retreated when attacked by the Mexican army during the Battle of Puebla.

**sovereignty (SOV-ren-tee)** The sovereignty of a country is its right to rule itself. When the French army invaded Mexico in 1862, the Mexican people believed their sovereignty was under threat, so they fought a war to kick the French army out of Mexico.

# Further Information

## Books

Behrens, June. *Fiesta!* Chicago: Children's Press, 1988.

Bradley, Mignon L. *Cinco de Mayo: An Historical Play.* Santa Barbara: Luisa Productions, 1981.

Palacios, Argentina. *Viva Mexico!: A Story of Benito Juárez and Cinco de Mayo.* Austin, Tex.: Steck-Vaughn, 1993.

Riehecky, Janet. *Cinco de Mayo.* Chicago: Children's Press, 1993.

## Web Sites

Visit our Web page for lots of links about Cinco de Mayo:
   *http://www.childsworld.com/links.html*

***Note to parents, teachers, and librarians: We routinely monitor our Web links to make sure they're safe, active sites.***

## Sources Used by the Author

Cadenhead, I. E. Jr. *Benito Juárez.* New York: Wayne Publication, Inc., 1993.

Gonzalez, Juan. *Harvest of Empire: A History of Latinos in America.* New York: Viking Penguin, 2000.

The Houston Public Library and Stafford Municipal School District. *Cinco de Mayo Page. www.hpl.lib.tx.us/youth/cinco_index.html*

Kanellos, Nicolás, with Cristelia Pérez. *Chronology of Hispanic-American History: From Pre-Columbian Times to the Present.* Detroit: Gale Research Inc., 1995.

Novas, Himilce. *Everything You Need to Know about Latino History.* New York: Plume, 1998.

Palacios, Argentina. *Viva Mexico! A Story of Benito Juárez and Cinco de Mayo.* Austin, Tex.: Steck-Vaughn Company, 1993.

Ruiz, Ramon Eduardo. *Triumphs and Tragedy.* New York: W. W. Norton & Company, 1992.